OnPage Search Engine Optimization Best Practices

By:

Dan Kerns

Copyright © 2017 Digital Marketing Web Design

Smashwords Edition, License Notes

This ebook is licensed for your personal enjoyment only. This ebook may not be re-sold or given away to other people. If you would like to share this book with another person, please purchase an additional copy for each recipient. If you're reading this book and did not purchase it, or it was not purchased for your enjoyment only, then please return to your favorite retailer and purchase your own copy. Thank you for respecting the hard work of this author.

What Is SEO and Why Is It Important?

What Are The Rules Of Onpage SEO?

Create A Catchy Title

Offer More Than Words

Get Keyword Placement Right

Time To Be Mobile Responsive

Include H1, H2, and Other Heading Tags

Optimize Your Page Load Speed

Building Authentic Connections

Proper Internal Linking Through Menu Navigation

Share On Social Media

Banish The Bounce

Write Entertaining Content

Start A Community

How Is Onpage SEO Changing?

About Me

References

For new businesses, the internet can feel like a vast and lawless place.

It represents a link to all the human knowledge that ever was or may be, so it's no exaggeration to say that finding a happy online home can be a challenge.

While there is no shortage of space out there, the challenge is learning how to build a sustainable, effective web presence.

To turn digital content into sales, businesses need to attract traffic [1]. They need to convince internet users that they have something valuable to offer and then lead them to it via the fastest route.

The greater the number of visitors means a higher chance of users reaching the end of the marketing funnel [2].

The funnel is the journey which a business wants visitors to make when they use their website. The end goal is not always a direct sale, but most companies are trying to convince people to make online purchases.

So, the objective is to get visitors to stick around long enough to want to buy something. Or, at the very least, decide to return a second, third, and fourth time [3].

Companies need to have an effective strategy to achieve this. With anywhere between 12-24 million online businesses in the world [4], how do users decide which ones are worth their time?

The answer is on-page SEO; the secret weapon of digital commerce.

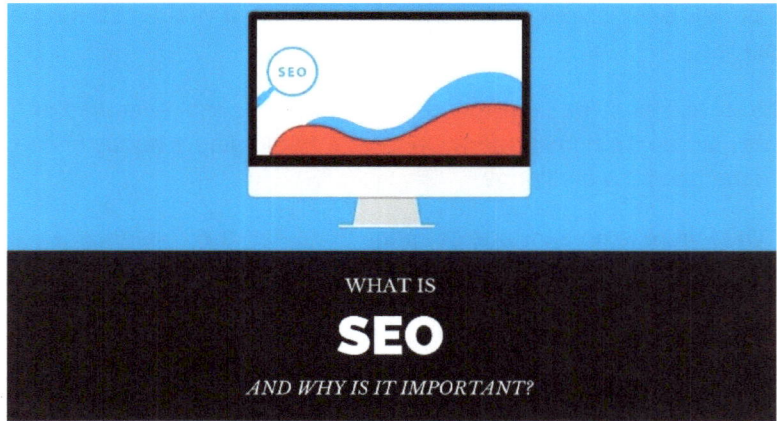

What Is SEO and Why Is It Important?

The first stage in mastering SEO, is to understand what it means. The basics are quite simple.

Often, they are needlessly complicated by technical jargon and algorithm data, but most businesses can do just fine without getting to grips with code.

It is important to know the rules of SEO and why they exist.

SEO (search engine optimization) is a series of algorithms and tools which search engines use to produce high quality results [5].

Every word and phrase typed into Google generates millions of results.

Theoretically, this should make finding valuable content impossible, but it does not. Google automatically arranges the results in order of their relevance.

When a user searches 'ladies shoes,' for example, the websites on the first page are not there by accident.

The top results have proven relevance, via onpage SEO and other factors considered. They have the best content for that particular search request.

The closer a website is to the top of the results page, there is more of a chance it will be selected by the user.

For this reason, SEO is the key to everything; traffic, sales, conversions, and online success [6].

In order to be found on the internet, businesses have to be easily read by SEO algorithms. There are different strategies to do this and onpage SEO optimization is one of the most effective.

The difference between 'onpage' and 'off page' is that the former involves changes made to the content itself, rather than external strategies to attract attention to it [7].

While algorithms are updated from time to time, the basic rules stay the same, so content creators can use them to climb up in the search results.

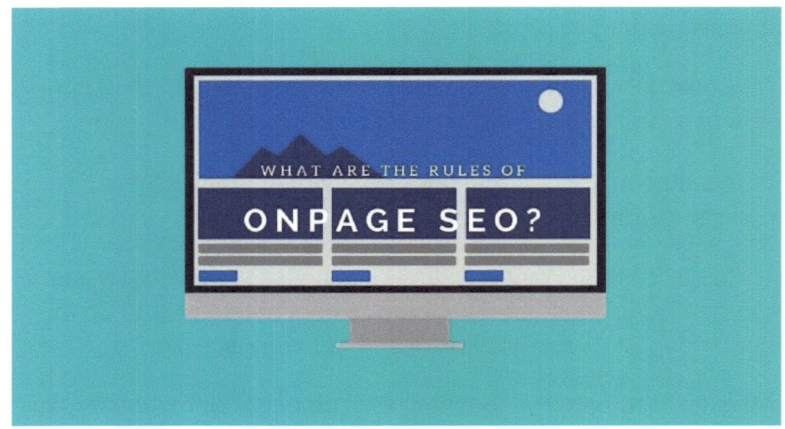

What Are the Rules of Onpage SEO?

It is best to approach content creation as the building of a virtual house.

Every piece of content or page is a new construction and must have standalone value, as well as connections to the rest.

The foundation is the bare bones content; the words of the article, blog, advertisement, or website description.

They may be high quality, but adding onpage SEO is the best way to ensure that they are valuable to the target market – and that they can found by this market.

The following SEO techniques represent virtual bricks.

Each one builds up the house and makes it stronger.

The content should be optimized without compromising its meaning or structure.

Create a Catchy Title

In many ways, the most influential onpage element is the title [8]. It is what every user sees first to determine whether the content is right for them.

It has to be interesting and catchy, because a boring title is off putting. However, it also has to demonstrate relevance and please the Google algorithms. The way to do this is to include a popular keyword, preferably at the beginning of the title [9].

This is not always possible, without making the words sound awkward, but the closer it is, the better the result.

For instance, 'Apple Pie in the Big Apple: Finding Great Desserts in New York' is a catchy title and it includes telling information; keywords (apple pie, desserts) and a location.

Remember that it is still better to include the keyword right at the end of the title than it is to omit it altogether.

Inclusion of the word 'great' in the above example demonstrates an easy way to boost its impact even further.

Many users enter single word searches into Google, but most focus on a string of words. Instead of just 'desserts,' they search for 'the best desserts' or 'great desserts near me.' These are known as long tail keywords. Modifiers (descriptive labels) are favored by Google, because they provide more information [10].

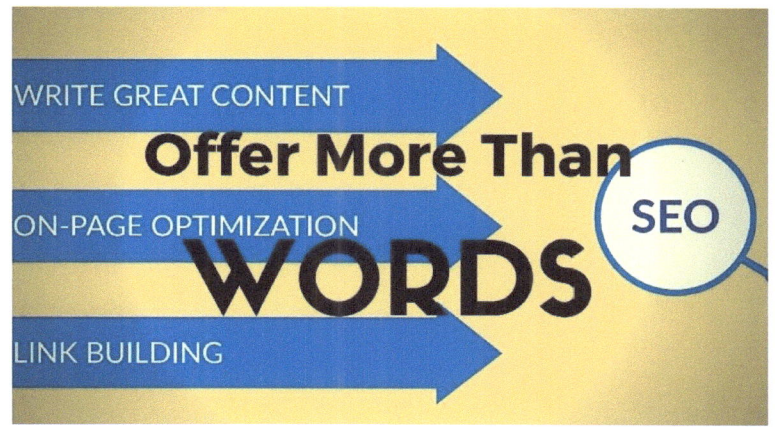

Offer More Than Words

The best online content is made up of more than just text.

The truth is that, no matter how valuable the words are, if they look boring on the page, people are unlikely to engage.

This is why the vast majority of website copy is short and sweet. It is visually broken down into sections, with the use of headings, subheadings, and bullet points.

Scrolling through pages and pages of unbroken text is something that most users just are not willing to do.

On the other hand, it is not true that longer content cannot drive traffic. It can actually provide greater value, because it provides more information. The problem is that getting people to stick around is harder.

Generally, a balance between brevity and depth is recommended.

If longer content is the only option or a business is confident that their target market wants in depth information, it should incorporate visual features.

Videos, images, and diagrams are a great way to break up the text and keep things fresh [11]. Infographics are a wonderful method of presenting complex or dense content. They combine key facts, figures, or insights with colorful graphics and a user friendly layout [12].

Get Keyword Placement Right

Keywords are the backbone of any good SEO strategy.

Google is very particular about how keywords are used. Of all their algorithm updates, most relate to keyword placement. It is because, theoretically, a content creator could stuff a website full of keywords. The content would, technically, be relevant because it contains a popular search term many times over [13].

However, it would not be valuable, precisely because it is made up of repeated phrases. Nobody wants to read keyword stuffed articles. They do not flow naturally and Google does not favor it.

What Google does favor is natural, intelligent keyword placement which makes contextual sense and does not seem like it has been placed there just for 'points.' Using a handful of popular keywords in a clever way is always better than throwing them in for effect.

For instance, make sure that the main keyword is included in the first 100-200 words [14]. This is one of the most common onpage SEO tips, because it is easy to do.

The placement of a single word or phrase can send content rising up in the search results. It tells users what is offered in the first or second paragraph. Google likes this, because it is an efficient system. All search engines want is to help people find relevant information.

The most popular content includes as many variations on the main keyword as is practically possible, without compromising contextual value. These are known as 'LSI keywords' (synonyms for the main one). The easiest way to find popular LSI options is to perform a search for the primary keyword. Then, scroll down to the bottom of the page and find the 'Searches Related To' section. These are the most influential variations [15].

Time to Be Mobile Responsive

Over the last five years, the demand for responsive websites has grown. In fact, it is generally agreed that all good content should now be fully optimized for a range of devices.

It is the only sensible approach when target markets are distributed across multiple viewing platforms. Some still surf the internet from a laptop or home computer. Others primarily browse using their smartphone or tablet [16].

There are so many internet ready devices that it would be impossible to construct different types of content for each one. However, website optimization gives content providers the chance to use an intelligent blueprint of sorts.

Content is applied to a changeable system which automatically responds to the user environment [17]. The resolution, image size, and scripting abilities are all determined by the method of access.

For example, an optimized and responsive website does not look the same when viewed on an iPad as it does on a computer. This is because the environments have unique needs.

Handheld devices are smaller, so they require bigger, brighter graphics. The configuration of images and words must be capable of shrinking to fit the screen size, without compromising the quality.

Include H1, H2, and Other Heading Tags for Proper On-Page SEO Optimization

So many content creators neglect H1 and H2 tags, but this is a mistake. They are easy to use and they contribute to onpage SEO.

Essentially, they do the same job as newspaper or magazine headlines. Think about how traditional print media gets people to stop and take an interest. It uses emotive words, bright colors, and catchy puns.

This kind of visual impact does not work for online content, because search engine results are just titles and snippets of text. It is why H1 and H2 tags were invented.

They are the coding equivalent of a big, loud headline. Placing them in certain parts of the text tells Google to make them stand out, because they are important [18].

Once again, Google favors content which willingly does this. It makes the job of organizing search results easier. Without tags, it takes longer to index the content and there is more chance of it being misinterpreted by the algorithm.

SEO tags are simple. The main title is heading 1 or H1 tag. The H2 tag works in exactly the same way, only it is arranged around the secondary titles or main subheading [19].

There are actually several more layers of tags that can be used, but most content includes just these first two, however it is recommended to utilize more heading tags for more in-depth content.

Including them is not going to produce amazing results, but it can provide quite a boost in some situations, particularly when combined with other on-page SEO techniques.

Optimize Your
PAGE LOAD SPEED

Optimize Your Page Load Speed

Onpage SEO optimization is about more than just content optimizing. It encompasses the whole website and the experience which it gives users. Think about the things that people want to get out of a visit. They want valuable content and useful information.

However, they are not usually willing to spend a great deal of time accessing it. There are millions of alternative options out there, so content has to be engaging and fast. Slow loading times are one of the most common reasons for high bounce rates.

This refers to users landing on a page and leaving within a few seconds. Websites with a low number of conversions need to take a look at their bounce rate [20]. It says a lot about what is happening and why visitors are not making it to the end of the funnel. Often, it is because pages take too long to load and they get bored and leave [21]. It is that simple.

Most never come back, so site speed should be a top priority. The internet is full of free performance checking tools, which can be used to determine current site speed [22].

If it is too slow, there are a number of ways to improve it, including compressing large images and switching to a better host. It is worth paying more for a host that is guaranteed to deliver consistent performance [23].

Build Authentic Connections

Many of these onpage SEO tips offer big results, for what amounts to small changes.

It does not take long to insert a keyword or to add H1 tags to a post. It gets even easier when content creators learn how to follow the rules instinctively.

Link building is a little different, however, because it takes more time. It depends upon constructive communication with other providers.

Outbound links are hyperlinks to the target website from another trusted source. Google adores them, because they function as a kind of endorsement [24]. If another website or blogger is willing to be associated with a piece of content, it must mean that they consider it valuable. After all, nobody would voluntarily endorse information that they do not like or trust.

Every outbound link is a vote of confidence and it pushes the target website up the search rankings. They are an effective, sustainable way to drive traffic.

The secret to success is careful consideration. The aim should always be to increase the quality of the content and this can only be done by creating virtual connections with relevant providers [25]. Acquiring links from just anybody is not the way to make this work.

Often, there is an exchange involved. Any website or blog with the potential to be a good affiliate will need a guarantee that linking out is beneficial for both parties. This might be as simple as agreeing to swap links, with each hosting one for the other [26]. Alternatively, some e-commerce businesses offer bloggers and reviewers free products in exchange for links. A good rule of thumb is to limit the number of links to four for every thousand words [27].

Proper Internal Linking Through Menu Navigation

The power of linking does not stop with third party endorsements. Internal links are valuable too. They have a direct impact on website navigation and make it easier for visitors to explore and find the information they need. This is important for onpage SEO as it contributes to the user experience [28]. The goal should be to give visitors a digital encounter which feels natural, enjoyable, and satisfying.

Rapid loading speeds, attractive images, and clear headings and titles are good ways to achieve it. Adding inbound links is like laying down a virtual path for website visitors. They are still in charge of where they end up, but they can now see all of the possible options.

Internal links are simple and just connect different pages. For example, on a website selling wooden floors, it would make sense to link to an internal page about wood maintenance.

It is best to pick linking opportunities carefully.

Just like keyword placement and outbound links, the focus should be on quality. The content will not benefit from this SEO strategy if every page is stuffed with irrelevant connections.

Aim to include two or three internal links per post or page. As the amount of content grows, linking will become easier. When a new page or post is added, it can be linked back to two or three older ones [29].

Share on Social Media

While social sharing buttons are not technically a part of the Google algorithms, they can give websites an extra boost. They show that internet users are enjoying and endorsing the content and Google rewards this interest. Facebook, Twitter, and Google+ all have sharing buttons, which can be inserted at the bottom or side of a page [30].

They are not intrusive and take up only a tiny amount of space. Plus, just one share or like from a satisfied visitor could bring a piece of content to the attention of hundreds more.

According to a recent study, placing social buttons in prominent places can increase the likelihood of shares by a staggering 700% [31]. It is all about making it easy for visitors to interact with a blog, article, review, or advertise.

Banish the Bounce

Bounce rate refers to how long visitors spend on a website after landing.

If the bounce rate is high, it means that some element is displeasing people and leading them to make a swift exit. The problem could be related to a number of things; from clunky navigation to slow loading times, poor quality content, unresponsive designs, and annoying features like pop ups [32].

High bounce rates lead to low conversions, because not enough users are making it through to the end of the marketing funnel. It is an issue which needs to be fixed and businesses can only do this by identifying the dysfunctional elements.

AB testing comes in very handy for this. All it means is that the content creator makes a change to the content (uses a different host, compresses images, writes in a different styles, etc.) and then records the results. The previous conditions are A and the new ones are B. They are compared to see if the change has fixed or improved upon the problem.

AB testing is highly recommended for all website alterations, no matter how small. It generates a history of development, which can be used to pinpoint design and content weaknesses [33]. Without a record, the only option is to repeatedly test every element of the platform, whenever traffic or conversions drop.

Google does consider bounce (or dwell) time when determining the quality of content [34]. While it is impossible to please everybody, only a small proportion of visitors should be landing on and leaving the website within a few seconds. It is important to put thought and time into content development, rather than just arranging onpage SEO around a piece of text. Make it entertaining, engaging, and capable of stimulating an emotional response.

Write Entertaining Content

It is worth spending some time talking about how to create engaging, valuable content.

It isn't always easy for businesses, particularly if they have no experience of technical or commercial writing. Nevertheless, many presume that they can handle it all 'in house.'

It saves money and the common misconception is that anybody can be a copywriter, so there should be nothing to stop a developer, designer, or manager from taking it on.

The truth is that copywriting is a precise skill.

Anybody can write, but it takes a certain degree of technical and creative proficiency to write in a way which pleases the Google algorithms [35].

Do not forget that the overarching goal for Google is to determine which pieces of content are the best. Quality is the top priority.

It is possible to incorporate all of these onpage SEO tips and still not rank highly, especially if the writing is poor or boring.

Online businesses are advised to either hire a skilled copywriter, with experience in their particular field, or receive comprehensive training for an internal employee.

Find a style and talk to the target market in a recognizable and fun, without being patronizing [36].

For example, an article targeted at middle aged men should look and flow very differently to a blog aimed at teenage girls.

It is acceptable to carry out research and observe the habits of rival companies. In fact, this kind of monitoring is standard practice for e-commerce businesses [37].

Content creators and developers often keep tabs on market rivals to make sure that they are not benefiting from techniques that have not even been considered.

Be careful never to explicitly copy, Google penalizes unoriginal content.

Start a Community

It took Google some time to confirm that it now considers things like blog and article comments when evaluating content. However, it has since championed the existence of what it calls 'thriving' online communities [38].

It is another example of how wide ranging onpage SEO can be. There are so many ways to give content a boost and they are not always restricted to a five hundred word piece on the 'best pizza in Manhattan' or the 'cheapest high heeled shoes.'

On the other hand, community is generated by high quality content.

It needs to be more than just a way to pass the time. If possible, try to write in a style which asks questions, because this is how you get people to comment [39].

It might be asking for opinions on a specific topic. It could be requesting personal experiences or encounters. Alternatively, content creators can encourage visitors to discuss the value of the article or blog itself [40].

Was it useful? Was it entertaining? Was it missing anything? The most fertile blog communities tend to be centered on big issues like politics, current affairs, and celebrity news.

The problem is that it is not always possible for a commercial enterprise, with a very specific agenda, to incorporate these things into their posts.

It is worth remembering though that even brief references to trending words and phrases will put content in front of larger audiences [41].

Two way engagements are a big part of maintaining a community, particularly on a loose form platform like a blog. Take time to respond to comments and questions from readers [42]. It is how relationships and connections are formed. The chance of a visitor returning to a website increases substantially if they have been made to feel like a part of something unique. It makes Google very happy too, because comments and extended interactions demonstrate value.

How is Onpage SEO Changing?

Just like everything else on the internet, onpage SEO exists in a state of perpetual change [43]. Usually, these shifts and tweaks are small, so content providers and creators can keep up.

If the rules were upended every time that a business figured out how to master them, they would not have any value. Things are changing, but the fundamental principles remain the same.

However, acknowledging and understanding algorithm developments can be a way to gain an edge on the competition.

The reason why Google constantly makes tweaks and changes is because it is trying to stay one step ahead of increasingly sophisticated online tools. With every new algorithm update, it gets harder for businesses to work the system.

If working the system is not an option, the only choice is to go back to basics and focus on quality and relevance; the root of all search engine algorithms.

It is worth pointing out though that some technological developments are already redefining SEO. Voice based searches have become very popular over the last three years, due to the release of intelligent OS like Siri and Cortana.

Eventually, voice based searching will start to erode the value of single keyword SEO, as people do not naturally speak using keywords. This is why companies are being encouraged to make a gradual shift towards long tailed phrases [44].

It is something that all good content providers incorporate anyway, but it is more important now than ever. Make it a goal to structure more keyword phrases around 'who, what, why, where, and how' queries.

The future belongs to those who can do more than just exploit onpage SEO.

It needs to be organic and instinctive. It should not be something that is checked off a tick list with every new piece of content, because skilled creators are able to adopt it as second nature.

This is how they end up with blogs and articles which sound warm and human.

It is vital that focus remains on the user.

While onpage SEO is designed to get the attention of a software algorithm, the end goal is always to engage the reader, visitor, or follower.

About Me

I own and operate [Digital Marketing Web Design](#), which is dedicated to helping business owners maximize their online presence through enhanced web design and marketing.

I offer a variety of stand-alone services as well as customized services tailored to individuals and their businesses.

I try to understand the problems that businesses face and do my best to help solve them.

I specialize in helping businesses optimize their in-house work flow as well as increase their online presence.

I enjoy figuring out how to make a situation better by identifying ways to solve problems while being as efficient as possible.

One of my favorite tasks I enjoy is assisting business owners with increasing their revenue through efficiency and optimization.

Another activity I enjoy is innovating ways to make money online.

For those wanting to contact me, I can be reached at dan@digitalmarketingwebdesign.com.

References:

[1] Mills, Ian (September 2, 2015) 'Five Reasons Website Traffic is the Lifeblood of Small Businesses'

http://www.huffingtonpost.com/ian-mills/5-reasons-website-traffic_b_6628080.html

[2] Lindner, Richard (July 30, 2015) 'How to Architect the Perfect Conversion Funnel for Your Business'

http://www.digitalmarketer.com/conversion-funnel/

[3] Gillick, Christina (March 3, 2014) 'A Simple Guide to Understanding and Creating a Website Conversion Funnel'

https://blog.crazyegg.com/2014/03/03/website-conversion-funnel/

[4] Paul, Ross (June 26, 2015) 'Just How Big is the E-Commerce Market?'

http://blog.lemonstand.com/just-how-big-is-the-ecommerce-market-youll-never-guess/

[5] Chris, Alex (Retrieved February 13, 2016) 'What Is Off Page SEO?'

https://www.reliablesoft.net/what-is-off-page-seo/

[6] Patel, Neil (Retrieved February 13, 2016) 'The On Page SEO Cheat Sheet'

http://neilpatel.com/blog/the-on-page-seo-cheat-sheet/

[7] Shengale, Ram (February 4, 2013) 'Off Page SEO for Beginners'

http://www.socialmediatoday.com/content/page-seo-beginners

[8] De Vaak, Joost (May 25, 2016) 'Crafting Good Titles for SEO'

https://yoast.com/page-titles-seo/

[9] Fergusson, Bill (January 26, 2016) 'The SEO Title Tag'

https://www.brightedge.com/blog/the-seo-title-tag/

[10] Miffsud, Justin (October 3, 2011) '15 Title Tag Optimization Guidelines for SEO'

http://usabilitygeek.com/15-title-tag-optimization-guidelines-for-usability-and-seo/

[11] Dean, Brian (October 8, 2016) 'On Page SEO: Anatomy of a Perfectly Optimised Page'

http://backlinko.com/on-page-seo

[12] Idijola, Victor (July 29, 2015) 'Why Infographics are the Secret to Super SEO'

https://thenextweb.com/insider/2015/07/29/why-infographics-are-the-secret-to-super-seo/#.tnw_F2xshx2U

[13] Agrawal, Harsh (January 8, 2016) 'What's the Optimum Keyword Density for Better Ranking?'

https://www.shoutmeloud.com/keyword-density-seo.html

[14] Gunelius, Susan (February 6, 2017) 'Tricks to Use Keyword In Your Blog Posts'

https://www.lifewire.com/tricks-to-use-keywords-in-blog-posts-3476654

[15] Halliur, Akshay (January 19, 2017) 'How to Find LSI Keywords and Smartly Implement Them for SEO'

https://www.gobloggingtips.com/lsi-keywords/

[16] Pilon, Annie (May 8, 2013) 'What is Responsive Web Design?'

https://smallbiztrends.com/2013/05/what-is-responsive-web-design.html

[17] Smashing Editorial (January 12, 2011) 'Responsive Web Design: What is It and How to Use It'

https://www.smashingmagazine.com/2011/01/guidelines-for-responsive-web-design/

[18] Jain, Gaurav (January 31, 2017) 'H1 and H2 Heading Tags for SEO

'http://www.emoneyindeed.com/h1-h2-heading-tags-seo-use/

[19] Parsons, James (September 16, 2014) 'The Proper Way to Use the Header Tag for SEO

'http://www.seoblog.com/2014/09/proper-way-use-header-tag-seo/

[20] Peyton, Jay (February 25, 2014) 'What is the Average Bounce Rate for a Website?'

http://www.gorocketfuel.com/the-rocket-blog/whats-the-average-bounce-rate-in-google-analytics/

[21] Labrador, Emma (December 24, 2015) 'Why Does Speed Page Impact Your SEO?'

https://www.semrush.com/blog/why-does-page-speed-impact-your-seo/

[22] Jackson, Brian (December 2, 2016) '16 Website Speed Test Tools for Analyzing Web Performance'

https://www.keycdn.com/blog/website-speed-test-tools/

[23] Armin, J (August 2, 2012) '15 Tips to Speed Up Your Website'

https://moz.com/blog/15-tips-to-speed-up-your-website

[24] Fishkin, Rand (February 24, 2009) '5 Reasons You Should Link Out to Others from Your Website'

https://moz.com/blog/5-reasons-you-should-link-out-to-others-from-your-website

[25] Bourn, Jennifer (November 8, 2013) '10 Ideas to Build Quality Inbound Links'

http://www.bourncreative.com/10-ideas-build-inbound-links-website-traffic/

[26] Lodico, Jim (December 27, 2010) '7 Ways to Improve Your Blog SEO with Inbound Links'

http://www.socialmediaexaminer.com/7-ways-to-improve-your-blog-seo-with-inbound-links/

[27] Northcutt, Corey (May 11, 2016) 'Inbound Link Building 101: 33 White Hat Ways to Build Backlinks for SEO'

https://blog.hubspot.com/blog/tabid/6307/bid/32479/32-white-hat-ways-to-build-inbound-links.aspx

[28] Labrador, Emma (January 28, 2016) 'Why Should You Focus on Internal Linking?'
http://positionly.com/blog/seo/internal-linking

[29] Crestodina, Andy (Retrieved on February 14, 2017) '3 Internal Linking Strategies for SEO and Conversions'

https://www.orbitmedia.com/blog/internal-linking/

[30] Redsicker, Patricia (February 24, 2014) '18 Social Media Resources to Improve Your Search Ranking'

http://www.socialmediaexaminer.com/social-media-seo/

[31] No Author (Retrieved February 13, 2017) 'The Anatomy of a Perfectly Optimized Page'

https://www.link-assistant.com/news/landing-page-optimization.html?fb_comment_id=1173159566049938_1344327462266480#f3a6ae170f20d1c

[32] Patel, Neil (Retrieved February 14, 2017) '13 Ways to Reduce Bounce Rate and Increase Your Conversions'

http://neilpatel.com/blog/13-ways-to-reduce-bounce-rate-and-increase-your-conversions/

[33] Saleh, Khalid (Retrieved February 13, 2017) 'How to Split Test Without Harming Your Site's SEO'

http://www.invespcro.com/blog/how-to-split-test-without-harming-your-sites-seo/

[34] Patel, Neil (June 11, 2014) 'Understanding the Impact of Dwell Time on SEO'

https://www.searchenginejournal.com/understanding-impact-dwell-time-seo/108905/

[35] Bigby, Garenne (October 31, 2016) '13 Avoidable Content Mistakes That Can Harm Your SEO'

https://dynomapper.com/blog/21-sitemaps-and-seo/244-13-avoidable-content-mistakes-that-can-harm-your-seo

[36] Dias, Nelson (August 7, 2016) '55 SEO Copywriting Tips for Rocking Content'

http://writtent.com/blog/35-seo-copywriting-tips-rocking-content/

[37] Weber, Irina (March 29, 2016) '15 Awesome Tools for SEO Competitor Analysis'

https://mention.com/blog/competitor-seo-tools/

[38] Slegg, Jennifer (April 27, 2016) 'Why Blog Comments Are Great for Google SEO'

http://www.thesempost.com/comments-good-for-google-seo/

[39] Harrold, Alyson (March 26, 2013) 'Blog Writing to Encourage Comments'

https://online-sales-marketing.com/blog-writing-encourage-comments/

[40] Urban, Diane (January 26, 2011) '9 Ways to Encourage People to Comment on Your Blog'

https://blog.hubspot.com/blog/tabid/6307/bid/8906/9-Ways-to-Encourage-People-to-Comment-on-your-Blog.aspx

[41] Price, Chuck (September 3, 2013) 'How to Use Google Trends for SEO'

https://searchenginewatch.com/sew/how-to/2292198/how-to-use-google-trends-for-seo

[42] Patel, Neil (August 20, 2014) 'Is It Worth Responding to Blog Comments?'

https://www.quicksprout.com/2014/08/20/is-it-worth-responding-to-blog-comments/

[43] Agrawal, AJ (March 14, 2016) 'According to the Experts, SEO is Changing'

http://www.inc.com/aj-agrawal/according-to-the-experts-how-seo-is-changing.html

[44] Peggs, Michael (January 6, 2017) 'How Voice Search is Changing SEO'

http://www.huffingtonpost.com/michael-peggs/how-voice-search-is-changing-seo_b_8926708.html

www.ingramcontent.com/pod-product-compliance
Lightning Source LLC
Chambersburg PA
CBHW041116180526
45172CB00001B/274